Turkey

Turkmenistan

Iraq

Afghanistan

Iran

Saudi
Arabia

# NAVID'S STORY...

## A real-life account of his journey from Iran

Created by
Andy Glynne
and Jonathan Topf

First published in 2015 by Wayland

Text and Illustrations © Mosaic Films 2015

Wayland, 338 Euston Road, London NW1 3BH

Wayland Australia, Level 17/207, Kent Street, Sydney, NSW 2000

Mosaic Films, Shacklewell Lane, London E8 2EZ

Created by Andy Glynne
Illustrated and designed by Jonathan Topf

Editor: Debbie Foy
Layout design: Sophie Wilkins

Dewey ref: 362.7'7914'092-dc23

ISBN 978 0 7502 7891 1
eBook ISBN 978 0 7502 9373 0
Lib eBook ISBN 978 0 7502 7896 6

Printed in China

10 9 8 7 6 5 4 3 2 1

Wayland is a division of Hachette Children's Books,
an Hachette UK company.

www.hachette.co.uk

# NAVID'S
## STORY...

My name is Navid.
This is the story of my
journey from Iran.

**WAYLAND**
www.waylandbooks.co.uk

The reason that we left Iran was that my dad disagreed
with the Government and how things were going.

I remember a visit from some Government officials one day.
My dad's life was in danger and so he had to leave the country immediately

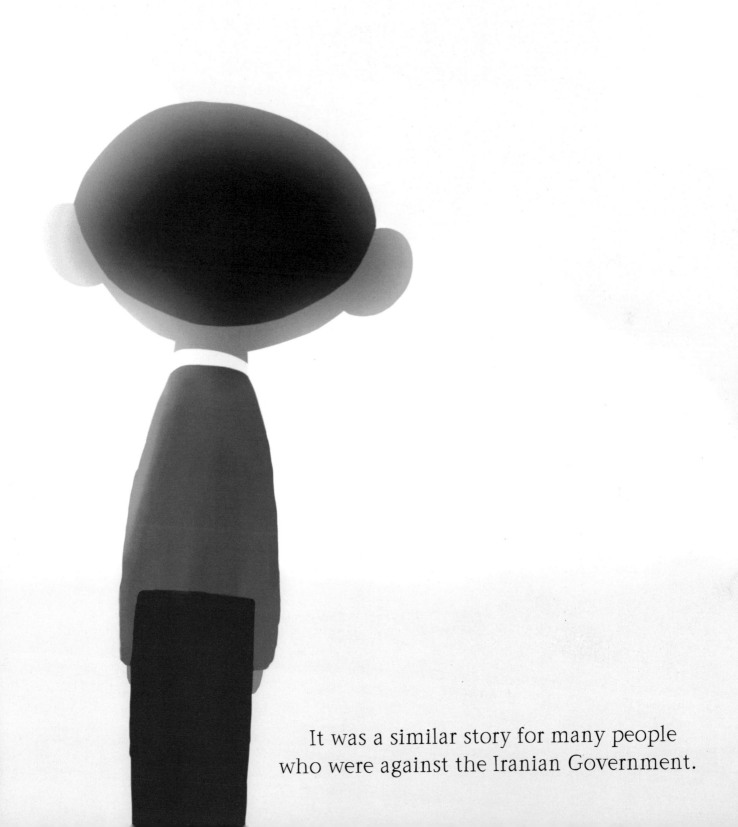

It was a similar story for many people
who were against the Iranian Government.

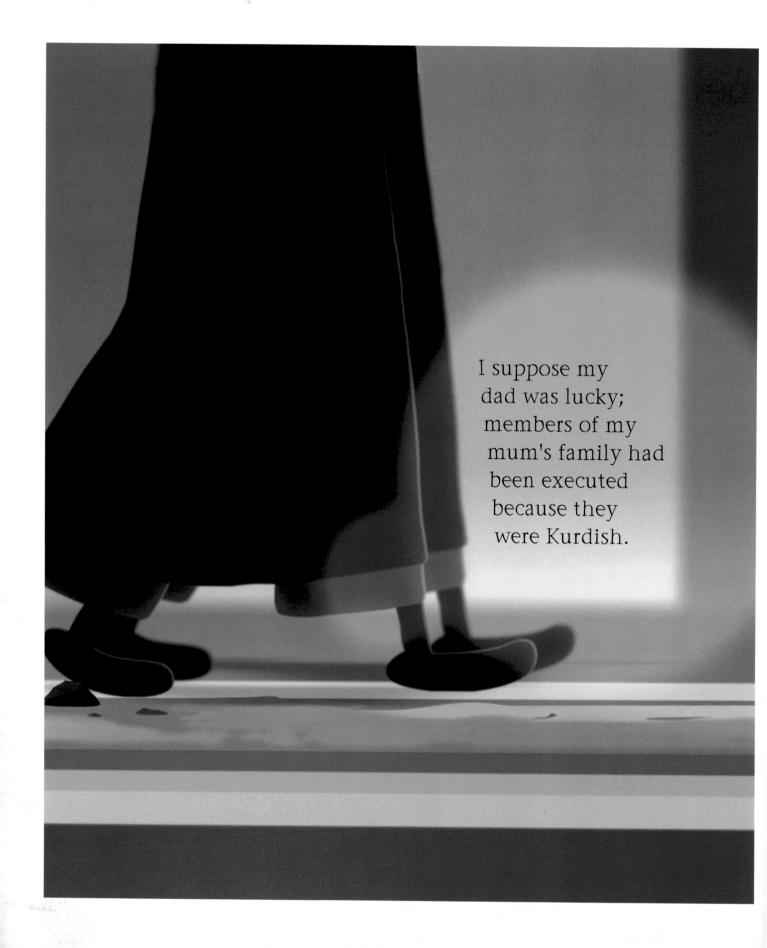

I suppose my dad was lucky; members of my mum's family had been executed because they were Kurdish.

After he left,
the officials kept coming
back to our house to question my
mum about where my dad had gone.

We decided we
had to leave too.

I remember everyone was really
sad the night we left Iran.

At first I didn't understand
why they were sad, but when I
got to the airport I realised that I
was leaving my country for good. I
was upset for nearly the whole journey.

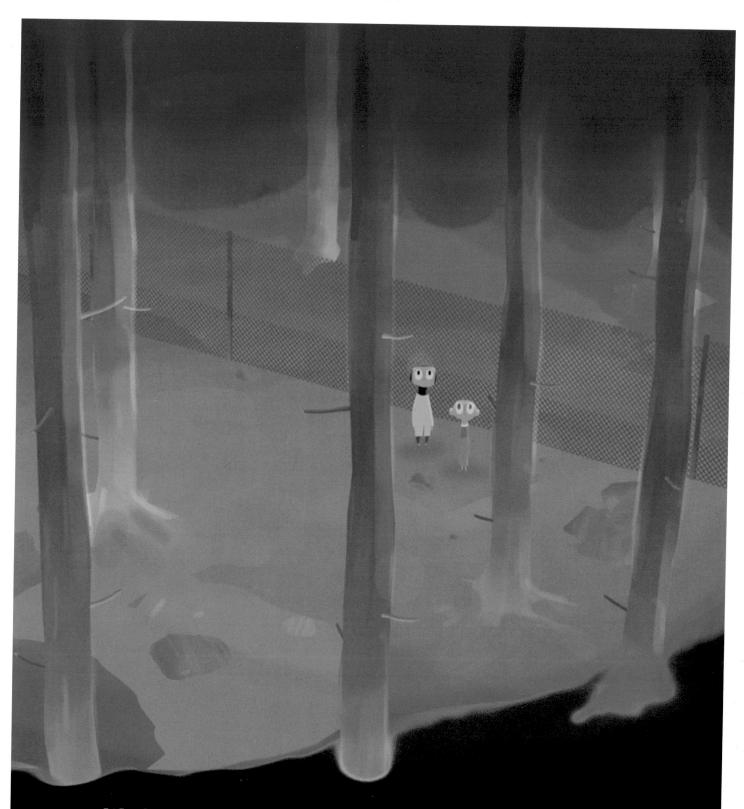

We flew to Italy and from there travelled mainly on foot.
We had to jump over a high wire fence, which was really scary.

We passed through a forest at night and got stopped by the local police. The sound of the police dog barking was terrifying.

I remember staying in a
cottage one night.
I think it was in Slovenia,
but I'm not sure.

The next night
when we had to
leave the cottage, I
was scared because
I could see the
concern on my
mum's face.

We climbed onto a lorry in France.

It was dark and uncomfortable.

I felt scared and really wanted to get out.

When we finally arrived in our new country, I remember someone cutting open the cover at the back of the lorry with a knife

It was just like in the movies,
when the sunlight flooded in to show
my mum and I sitting there huddled
up at the back of the lorry.

When we got out of the lorry the border officials questioned us, but they were really friendly.

That was the day that I saw my dad for the first time in several years.

It was the weirdest thing because
it wasn't what I was expecting at all.

At first I didn't recognise him,
but then he explained that he was my
dad and how he'd missed me so much.

I remember sitting in the back of the car,
my mum and dad were in the front.

It was night time and I spent the whole
journey looking at him, trying to figure out
who he was and what was happening.

But gradually,

I became more and more comfortable around
him as I figured out that he was actually my dad!

I started school in my new country.
The first few days were really hard,
  not because of the other students or teachers,
    but just because I didn't know anything
      – not even the language.

It was like being an
outsider, and that was
really scary for me.

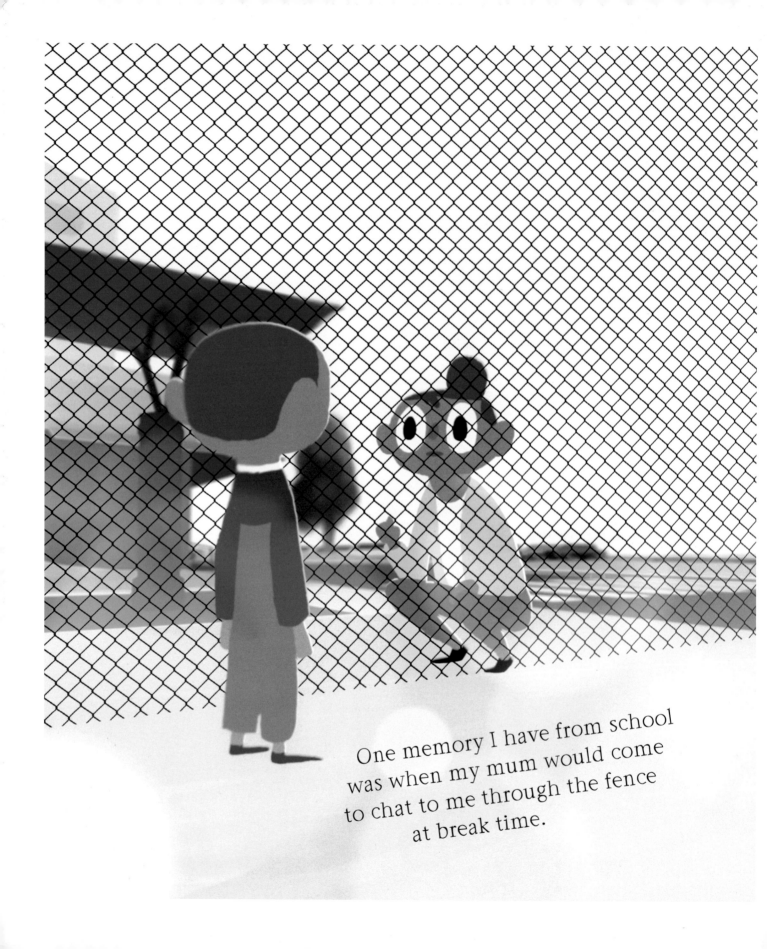

One memory I have from school was when my mum would come to chat to me through the fence at break time.

When the bell rang to go back to classes, my mum had to go home, but I held on to the school fence as though I was in some sort of prison.

I couldn't
understand
much of what was
said to me at school.
I just felt very
lonely.

You could tell by their facial expressions that people were being friendly, but not knowing what they were saying was quite scary for me.

School was pretty difficult for me at first.

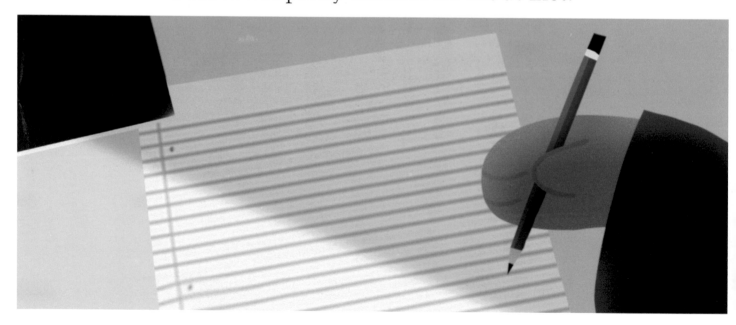

I had to learn to do everything.

At my school there was a wide variety of kids from different backgrounds.

There were other refugee kids at my school,
    and there was a centre you could go to after school
        to be with other kids in similar situations.

We could share our experiences and this was helpful for me.

So even though the first few months
were difficult, having that sense of
support was amazing for me.

And, of course, I had my mum and dad.

The complete **SEEKING REFUGE** series.

Real-life testimonies of young refugees fleeing their homelands.

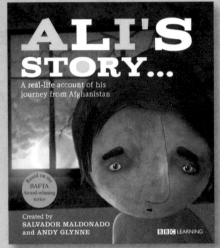

9780750278874
eBk ISBN 978 0 7502 9337 2

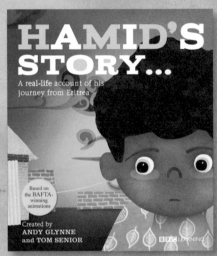

9780750278904
eBk ISBN 978 0 7502 9348 8

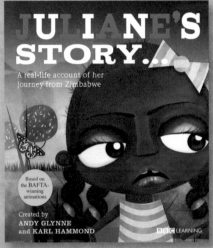

9780750278898
eBk ISBN 978 0 7502 9347 1

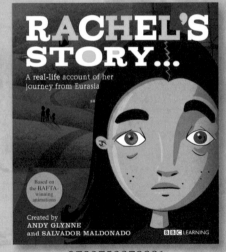

9780750278881
eBk ISBN 978 0 7502 9374 7

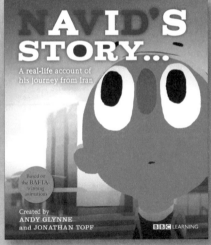

9780750278911
eBk ISBN 978 0 7502 9373 0

Available only from WAYLAND

WAYLAND
www.waylandbooks.co.uk